# moroccan

# moroccan

AROMATIC AND SPICY RECIPES
FROM A CLASSIC CUISINE

introduction by
rebekah hassan

southwater

This edition is published by Southwater
Southwater is an imprint of Anness Publishing Ltd
Hermes House, 88–89 Blackfriars Road, London SE1 8HA
tel. 020 7401 2077; fax 020 7633 9499
www.southwaterbooks.com; info@anness.com
© Anness Publishing Ltd 1999, 2004 , 2005

UK agent: The Manning Partnership Ltd, 6 The Old Dairy, Melcombe Road, Bath BA2 3LR; tel. 01225 478444; fax 01225 478440;
sales@manning-partnership.co.uk
UK distributor: Grantham Book Services Ltd, Isaac Newton Way, Alma Park Industrial Estate, Grantham, Lincs NG31 9SD; tel. 01476 541080; fax
01476 541061; orders@gbs.tbs-ltd.co.uk
North American agent/distributor: National Book Network, 4501 Forbes Boulevard, Suite 200, Lanham, MD 20706; tel. 301 459 3366;
fax 301 429 5746; www.nbnbooks.com
Australian agent/distributor: Pan Macmillan Australia, Level 18, St Martins Tower, 31 Market St, Sydney, NSW 2000; tel. 1300 135 113;
fax 1300 135 103; customer.service@macmillan.com.au
New Zealand agent/distributor: David Bateman Ltd, 30 Tarndale Grove, Off Bush Road, Albany, Auckland; tel. (09) 415 7664; fax (09) 415 8892

A CIP catalogue record for this book is available from the British Library.

*Publisher* Joanna Lorenz
*Senior Cookery Editor* Linda Fraser
*Project Editor* Zoe Antoniou
*Designer* Ian Sandom
*Illustrations* Madeleine David
*Photographers* William Adams-Lingwood, Karl Adamson, James Duncan, Michelle Garrett, Amanda Heywood, Don Last, Patrick McLeavey
and Michael Michaels
*Recipes* Jacqueline Clark, Roz Denny, Matthew Drennan, Joanna Farrow, Christine France, Carole Handslip, Chris Ingram, Soheila Kimberley,
Patricia Lousada, Sue Maggs, Maggie Pannell and Liz Trigg
*Food for photography* Carla Capalbo, Katherine Hawkins, Lucy McKelvie, Jane Stevenson and Elizabeth Wolf-Cohen
*Stylists* Madelaine Brehaut, Marion McLornan and Fiona Tillet
*Cover Photography* Nicki Dowey, *Food Stylist* Emma Patmore, *Design* Wilson Harvey

Previously published as part of the *Classic* cookery series

1 3 5 7 9 10 8 6 4 2

For all recipes, quantities are given in both metric and imperial measures, and, where appropriate, measures are also given in
standard cups and spoons. Follow one set, but not a mixture, because they are not interchangeable.

Picture on frontispiece shows a selection of dried ingredients and spices.

# CONTENTS

# INTRODUCTION

For many people, Moroccan food is an unknown quantity. There are few Moroccan restaurants outside Morocco, and even in the country itself restaurants are a rare sight. However, Moroccan food is one of the country's undeniable delights. In terms of subtlety, delicacy and flavour, it can be compared with the much more famous cuisines of France, India and China.

Morocco has been subject to a huge range of influences over the centuries, through trade as well as invasion. The indigenous people are the Berbers, a non-Arab race who have lived a simple rural life and inhabited North Africa since the earliest recorded time. Many of the Berber dishes have been passed down the female line of the family by word of mouth (it is always women who are to be found in a Moroccan kitchen), by mothers, aunts and grandmothers. This has preserved many important recipes that would otherwise have been lost in a language that is almost completely spoken.

The most famous of all Berber dishes is couscous – the national dish of Morocco. The word gives its name both to the dish itself and to the granules of semolina that form the basis of this speciality. It is ideal served with the gravy of the tagine, a thick stew of meat and vegetables that is also a popular Berber dish.

When the Arabs invaded Morocco in 682, they brought with them a different culture and religion – Islam. Eating customs and ingredients were also different. As the Arabs conquered Persia, Syria, Egypt and later India, Indonesia and China, foods and dishes arrived in Morocco from the East. Spices, like ginger, saffron, turmeric and – perhaps most important of all – cinnamon, became a central part of Moroccan cooking.

New ingredients and cooking methods also arrived with the Bedouins (whose name means "dwellers of the desert"), the nomadic Arabs who moved into Morocco from the eleventh century onwards. Their diet included dates, milk and bread. Other influences found their way across the Mediterranean as the conquering Arabs made their way to Spain, where fruit and vegetables had arrived from America.

Moroccan meals are usually served at low round tables. A simple meal might comprise one or two tagines, served with raw and cooked salads. For special occasions, a couscous is served. Bread is always served, and a meal would be considered incomplete without it. Mint tea is another essential part of Moroccan life. This drink was introduced as recently as the 1800s, but it is now served all over Morocco.

*The picture shows a selection of succulent Moroccan baked dishes (clockwise from top): Little Spiced Breads, Serpent Cake and Briouates with Almonds and Dates.*

# INGREDIENTS

**ALMONDS** These can be blanched and used whole, chopped or flaked and then toasted and/or ground for fillings or stuffings.

**CHARMOULA** Moroccan cooks almost always use this marinade when cooking fish. It usually includes garlic, cumin, paprika, cayenne pepper, fresh parsley and coriander, white wine vinegar, lemon juice and olive oil.

**CHICK-PEAS** These are extremely popular in Morocco, where they are used in soups, tagines and couscous dishes and are sold in the markets loose by the kilo. Moroccans would never use canned chick-peas. However, although the texture isn't the same, canned chick-peas can be used for speed and ease.

**CINNAMON** This spice is widely used in Moroccan cookery. It is added to soups and tagines, and fried pastries are commonly dusted with icing sugar and ground cinnamon. Sticks give a more subtle flavour, but ground cinnamon is used more often in cooking.

*Favourite Moroccan ingredients include (clockwise from left): Couscous; blanched, whole, flaked and shelled almonds; dried chick-peas and ground almonds (centre).*

*A bowl of marinated olives is a welcome addition to any meal.*

**CORIANDER** Another essential ingredient in Moroccan cookery, coriander adds a wonderful pungency to dishes and, like parsley, is often used in large quantities. Buy it pre-packed in supermarkets or loose in ethnic shops.

**COUSCOUS** Most of the couscous available in supermarkets is the pre-cooked variety, which can be prepared quickly by steaming or soaking in boiling water or stock. Uncooked couscous is less readily available and is more complicated to cook, although the end result is good. Couscous may be cooked in a couscousier, a type of double saucepan in which a stew is simmered in the bottom half and the couscous is steamed in the top.

**CUMIN** Used frequently in soups and tagines, cumin is especially popular in fish and poultry dishes. Grind the seeds in a pestle and mortar, or simply buy the spice ready-ground.

**GINGER** This fragrant spice has a slightly hot, peppery taste. It is frequently used with paprika and black pepper, which contrast with its underlying sweetness. Ground ginger adds a more mellow flavour than the fresh root and is more commonly used by Moroccan cooks.

*Preserved lemons are stored in salt, so rinse before use.*

**HARISSA** Occasionally, Moroccan dishes are spiced with harissa, a hot chilli paste from Algeria. Use it with caution, particularly if you are unfamiliar with it, as it is quite fiery. Always add a little at a time, to suit your taste. If it is not available, use a few drops of Tabasco sauce as a substitute.

**HONEY** Moroccans have a very sweet tooth and use honey lavishly, not only in sweet dishes but in savoury ones as well. Moroccan honey is thick, with an aromatic, herbal flavour. Greek honey made from the nectar of thyme and rosemary flowers makes a good substitute.

**OLIVES** There are three main types of olives used in Moroccan cookery: unripe green olives, used mostly in salads; ripe, tan-coloured olives, which range in colour from deep green through to rose, violet or dark red; and black olives that have been cured in salt. Marinated olives are also delicious and can be found in various ethnic stores.

**PAPRIKA** This is hugely popular and used in numerous dishes. It is an essential element in charmoula and is also used in salads and tagines. As with all peppers and hot sauces, add a little at a time to suit your tastes.

**PARSLEY** In Morocco, parsley is used far more as a vegetable than as a herb so use generously. Try to use flat leaf parsley, which has a mild, fragrant flavour, if you can find it.

**CAYENNE PEPPER** This fiery spice is popular in southern parts of Morocco, where food is more highly spiced.

**BLACK PEPPER** Add piquancy to savoury dishes with freshly ground black peppercorns rather than using ready-ground pepper, as this will make the flavour more pungent.

**SAFFRON** Although a relatively expensive spice, small amounts of saffron are used extensively in Moroccan cookery, adding colour and a subtle aroma to dishes. Grind the threads in a pestle and mortar or soak to make saffron water.

**TURMERIC** Although it is sometimes used instead of saffron, turmeric is also an important spice in its own right, adding pungency and colour to soups.

*Above (clockwise from the top): cumin seeds, saffron threads, cayenne pepper, ground turmeric, cinnamon sticks, ground cinnamon, paprika, black peppercorns, ground cumin and ground ginger (centre).*

# HARIRA

his hearty soup is eaten during the month of Ramadan, when Muslims fast between sunrise and sunset.

INGREDIENTS

*450g/1lb well-flavoured tomatoes*
*225g/8oz lamb, cut into 1cm/½in pieces*
*2.5ml/½ tsp ground turmeric*
*2.5ml/½ tsp ground cinnamon*
*25g/1oz/2 tbsp butter*
*60ml/4 tbsp chopped fresh coriander*
*30ml/2 tbsp chopped fresh parsley*
*1 onion, chopped*
*50g/2oz/¼ cup split red lentils*
*75g/3oz/½ cup dried chick-peas,*
*soaked overnight*
*4 baby onions or small shallots, peeled*
*25g/1oz/¼ cup soup noodles*
*salt and freshly ground black pepper*
*chopped fresh coriander, lemon slices and*
*ground cinnamon, to garnish*

SERVES 4

COOK'S TIP
Dried chick-peas are available in most supermarkets and health food stores. If you prefer, use a drained can of chick-peas instead.

1 Plunge the tomatoes into a bowl of boiling water for 30 seconds, then refresh in cold water. Peel away the skins. Cut into quarters and remove the seeds. Chop roughly.

2 Put the lamb, turmeric, ground cinnamon, butter, coriander, parsley and onion into a large pan, and cook over a moderate heat, stirring, for 5 minutes. Add the chopped tomatoes and continue to cook for 10 minutes.

3 Rinse the split red lentils under cold running water and add to the saucepan along with the drained chick-peas and 600ml/1 pint/2½ cups water. Season with salt and pepper. Bring to the boil, cover, and simmer gently for 1½ hours.

4 Add the baby onions or shallots and cook for a further 30 minutes. Add the soup noodles 5 minutes before the end of this cooking time. Garnish with the coriander, lemon slices and cinnamon.

# CHICK-PEA AND PARSLEY SOUP

 resh parsley gives this soup a deliciously fresh taste – to make a vegetarian version, just use a vegetable instead of a chicken stock.

INGREDIENTS
*225g/8oz/1⅓ cups chick-peas,
soaked overnight
1 small onion
1 bunch fresh parsley, about 40g/1½oz
30ml/2 tbsp olive and sunflower
oil, mixed
1.2 litres/2 pints/5 cups chicken stock
juice of ½ lemon
salt and freshly ground black pepper
lemon wedges and finely pared strips of
rind, to garnish
Moroccan Bread, to serve*

SERVES 6

1 Drain the chick-peas and rinse under cold water. Cook in boiling water for 1–1½ hours until tender. Drain and peel the chick-peas by rubbing the outer skins away with your fingers.

2 Place the onion and parsley in a food processor or blender and process until finely chopped.

3 Heat the olive and sunflower oils in a large saucepan or flameproof casserole and fry the onion and parsley mixture for about 4 minutes over a low heat until the onion is slightly softened.

4 Add the peeled chick-peas, cook gently for 1–2 minutes and add the chicken stock. Season well with salt and pepper. Bring the soup to the boil, then cover and simmer for 20 minutes until the chick-peas are very tender.

5 Allow the soup to cool a little and then part-purée in a food processor or blender, or by mashing the chick-peas fairly roughly with a fork, so that the soup is thick but still quite chunky.

6 Return the soup to a clean saucepan, add the lemon juice and adjust the seasoning if necessary. Heat gently and then serve garnished with lemon wedges and finely pared rind, and accompanied by Moroccan Bread.

# GARLIC PRAWNS

This truly delicious starter can be prepared in moments. Make sure you use fresh raw prawns which absorb the flavours of the garlic and chilli as they fry. Have everything ready for last minute cooking so you can take it to the table still sizzling.

### INGREDIENTS
*350–450g/12oz–1lb large raw prawns*
*2 red chillies*
*75ml/5 tbsp olive oil*
*3 garlic cloves, crushed*
*salt and freshly ground black pepper*

*SERVES 4*

1 Remove the heads and shells from the prawns, leaving the tails intact. Rinse them quickly under cold water and pat dry.

2 Halve each chilli lengthways and discard the seeds. Heat the oil in a flameproof pan, suitable for serving. (Alternatively, use a frying pan and have a warmed serving dish ready in the oven.)

3 Add all the prawns, chilli and garlic to the pan and cook over a high heat for about 3–4 minutes, stirring until the prawns turn pink. Season lightly with salt and pepper and serve immediately.

# MEAT BRIOUATES

he Moroccans enjoy the taste of sweet and savoury together, and they traditionally sprinkle these little pastry snacks with ground cinnamon and icing sugar. It is an unusual but delicious combination.

### INGREDIENTS
*175g/6oz filo pastry*
*40g/1½oz/3 tbsp butter, melted*
*sunflower oil, for frying*
*fresh flat leaf parsley, to garnish*
*ground cinnamon and icing sugar,*
*to garnish (optional)*

### FOR THE MEAT FILLING
*30ml/2 tbsp sunflower oil*
*1 onion, finely chopped*
*1 small bunch fresh coriander, chopped*
*1 small bunch fresh parsley, chopped*
*375g/12oz lean minced beef or lamb*
*2.5ml/½ tsp paprika*
*5ml/1 tsp ground coriander*
*good pinch of ground ginger*
*2 eggs, beaten*

*MAKES ABOUT 24*

1 First make the filling. Heat the oil in a frying pan and fry the onion and herbs over a low heat for about 4 minutes until the onion is softened. Add the meat and cook for about 5 minutes, stirring frequently, until the meat is evenly browned and most of the moisture has evaporated.

2 Drain away any excess fat and stir in the spices. Cook for 1 minute, remove the pan from the heat and stir in the beaten eggs. Stir until they begin to set and resemble lightly scrambled eggs. Set aside.

3 Take a sheet of filo pastry and cut into 8.5cm/3½in strips. Cover the remaining pastry with clear film to prevent it drying out. Brush a pastry strip with melted butter, then place a heaped teaspoon of the meat filling at one end of the strip, about 1cm/½in from the end. Fold one corner over the filling to make a triangular shape.

4 Fold the "triangle" over itself and then continue to fold, keeping the triangle shape, until you reach the end of the strip. Continue in this way until all the mixture has been used up.

5 Heat about 1cm/½in oil in a heavy-based pan and fry the Briouates in batches for 2–3 minutes until golden, turning once. Drain on kitchen paper and arrange on a serving plate. Serve garnished with fresh parsley and sprinkle with ground cinnamon and icing sugar, if liked.

# BYESAR

he Arab dish Byesar is similar to Middle Eastern hummus but uses broad beans instead of chick-peas. In Morocco it is eaten by dipping fresh bread into ground spices and then scooping up the purée.

## INGREDIENTS
*115g/4oz dried broad beans, soaked and drained*
*2 garlic cloves, peeled*
*5ml/1 tsp cumin seeds*
*about 60ml/4 tbsp olive oil*
*salt, to taste*
*fresh mint sprigs and cayenne pepper, to garnish*
*cumin seeds and bread, to serve (optional)*

*SERVES 4–6*

1 Put the soaked and drained broad beans in a pan with the whole garlic cloves and cumin seeds and add enough water just to cover. Bring to the boil, then reduce the heat and simmer until the beans are tender. Drain, cool and then slip off the outer skin of each bean.

2 Process the broad beans in a blender or food processor, gradually adding the olive oil and a little water as needed until the dip is soft and smooth. Season to taste with plenty of salt. Garnish with sprigs of fresh mint and cayenne pepper, then serve with cumin seeds and bread, if liked.

# SPICED AUBERGINE SALAD

erve this salad with warm pitta bread as a starter or to accompany a main course couscous.

### INGREDIENTS
*2 small aubergines*
*75ml/5 tbsp olive oil*
*50ml/2fl oz/¼ cup red wine vinegar*
*2 garlic cloves, crushed*
*15ml/1 tbsp lemon juice*
*2.5ml/½ tsp ground cumin*
*2.5ml/½ tsp ground coriander*
*½ cucumber, thinly sliced*
*2 well-flavoured tomatoes, thinly sliced*
*30ml/2 tbsp natural yogurt*
*salt and freshly ground black pepper*
*chopped flat leaf parsley, to garnish*

### SERVES 4

1 Preheat the grill. Cut the aubergines into slices and brush lightly with some of the olive oil. Cook them under a high heat, turning once, until golden and tender.

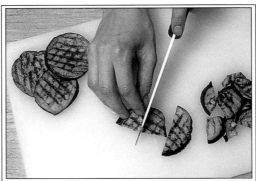

2 Remove the slices from the grill and cut them into quarters.

3 Mix together the remaining oil, vinegar, garlic, lemon juice, cumin and coriander in a bowl. Season with salt and pepper and mix thoroughly.

4 Add the warm aubergines, stir the mixture well and chill for at least 2 hours, preferably overnight. Add the cucumber and tomatoes and mix gently. Transfer to a serving dish and spoon the yogurt on top. Sprinkle with as much chopped parsley as you like.

# CHICKEN COUSCOUS

**T**he chicken and couscous can both be cooked the day before and then reheated for serving.

### INGREDIENTS
*8 chicken legs (thighs and drumsticks)*
*30ml/2 tbsp olive oil*
*1 onion, finely chopped*
*2 garlic cloves, crushed*
*5ml/1 tsp ground turmeric*
*2.5ml/½ tsp ground ginger*
*2.5ml/½ tsp ground cinnamon*
*450ml/¾ pint/scant 2 cups chicken stock*
*150g/5oz/1¼ cups stoned green olives*
*1 lemon, sliced*
*salt and freshly ground black pepper*
*fresh coriander sprigs, to garnish*

### FOR THE VEGETABLE COUSCOUS
*600ml/1 pint/2½ cups chicken stock*
*450g/1lb/2⅔ cups couscous*
*4 courgettes, thickly sliced*
*2 carrots, thickly sliced*
*2 small turnips, peeled and cubed*
*45ml/3 tbsp olive oil*
*450g/15oz can chick-peas, drained*
*15ml/1 tbsp chopped coriander*

*SERVES 8*

1 Preheat the oven to 180°C/350°F/Gas 4. Cut the legs in two through the joint.

2 Heat the oil in a large flameproof casserole and, working in batches, brown the chicken on both sides. Remove and keep warm.

3 Add the onion and crushed garlic to the flameproof casserole and cook gently until tender. Add the spices and cook for 1 minute. Pour over the stock, bring to the boil, and return the chicken. Cover and bake for 45 minutes until tender.

4 Transfer the chicken to a bowl, cover and keep warm. Remove any fat from the cooking liquid and boil to reduce by one-third. Meanwhile, blanch the olives and lemon slices in a pan of boiling water for 2 minutes until the lemon skin is tender. Drain and add to the cooking liquid, adjusting the seasoning to taste.

5 To cook the couscous, bring the second batch of chicken stock to the boil in a large pan and sprinkle in the couscous slowly. Stir all the time. Remove from the heat, cover and leave to stand for 5 minutes.

6 Meanwhile, cook the vegetables in a pan of boiling water, drain and put in a large bowl. Add the couscous and oil and season. Stir the grains to fluff them up, add the chick-peas and the chopped coriander. Spoon on to a large serving plate, cover with the chicken pieces, and spoon over the liquid. Garnish with fresh coriander sprigs.

# COUSCOUS AROMATIQUE

little harissa paste stirred in at the end of the cooking time adds a wonderful zing to this tasty vegetable couscous.

### INGREDIENTS

*450g/1lb/2⅔ cups couscous*
*60ml/4 tbsp olive oil*
*1 onion, cut in chunks*
*2 carrots, cut in thick slices*
*4 baby turnips, halved*
*8 small new potatoes, halved*
*1 green pepper, cut in chunks*
*115g/4oz green beans, halved*
*1 small fennel bulb, sliced thickly*
*2.5cm/1in cube fresh root ginger, grated*
*2 garlic cloves, crushed*
*5ml/1 tsp ground turmeric*
*15ml/1 tbsp ground coriander*
*5ml/1 tsp cumin seeds*
*5ml/1 tsp ground cinnamon*
*45ml/3 tbsp red lentils*
*400g/14oz can chopped tomatoes*
*1 litre/1¾ pints/4 cups stock*
*60ml/4 tbsp raisins*
*rind and juice of 1 lemon*
*harissa paste (optional)*
*salt and freshly ground black pepper*

*SERVES 4–6*

1 Cover the couscous with cold water and leave for 10 minutes. Drain and spread on a tray for 20 minutes, stirring occasionally.

2 In a large saucepan, heat the olive oil and fry all the chopped vegetables for about 10 minutes, stirring from time to time.

3 Add the fresh ginger, garlic and spices, stir well and cook for 2 minutes. Pour in the lentils, tomatoes, stock and raisins, and add seasoning to taste. Bring to the boil, then lower the heat to a simmer.

4 Place the couscous in a steamer and fit this on top of the stew. Cover and steam gently for 20 minutes until soft. Fork through, season and place in a serving dish.

5 Add the lemon rind and juice to the stew, and check the seasoning. Add a little harissa paste to taste, if liked. Put the couscous on to a plate and add some stew.

# SEA BASS AND FENNEL TAGINE

T his is a delicious tagine where the fish is flavoured with charmoula, a favourite blend of herbs and spices.

INGREDIENTS

*675g/1½lb sea bass, monkfish or cod fillets*
*225g/8oz raw Mediterranean prawns*
*30ml/2 tbsp olive oil*
*1 onion, chopped*
*1 fennel bulb, sliced*
*225g/8oz small new potatoes, halved*
*475ml/16fl oz/2 cups fish stock*
*lemon wedges, to serve (optional)*

FOR THE CHARMOULA

*2 garlic cloves, crushed*
*20ml/4 tsp ground cumin*
*20ml/4 tsp paprika*
*pinch of chilli powder or cayenne pepper*
*30ml/2 tbsp chopped fresh parsley*
*30ml/2 tbsp chopped fresh coriander*
*45ml/3 tbsp white vinegar*
*15ml/1 tbsp lemon juice*

SERVES 4

1 Skin the fish if necessary and remove any bones, then cut into large bite-size chunks. Top and tail the prawns and pull away the shells. Cut along the back of each prawn and remove the dark thread.

2 Make the charmoula by blending all the ingredients together in a bowl.

3 Place the fish fillets and prawns in two separate shallow dishes. Add half the charmoula marinade to each dish and stir well to coat the fish evenly. Cover with clear film and set aside in a cool place for about 30 minutes to 2 hours.

4 Heat the oil in a large flameproof casserole and fry the chopped onion for 2 minutes. Add the fennel and continue cooking over a gentle heat for 5–6 minutes until the onion and fennel are flecked with brown. Add the potatoes and fish stock and cook for a further 10–15 minutes until the potatoes are tender.

5 Add the marinated fish, stir gently and cook for 4 minutes, then add the prawns and all the remaining marinade and cook for a further 5–6 minutes until the fish is tender and the prawns are pink.

6 Serve in bowls, with lemon wedges for squeezing, if liked.

21

# LAMB TAGINE WITH COUSCOUS

 tagine is a Moroccan stew that typically combines meat and fruit with aromatic herbs and spices.

INGREDIENTS
*15ml/1 tbsp sunflower oil*
*350g/12oz lean, boneless lamb, cubed*
*1 large onion, chopped*
*1 garlic clove, crushed*
*600ml/1 pint/2½ cups stock*
*1 cinnamon stick*
*small piece of fresh root ginger, peeled and finely chopped*
*5ml/1 tsp clear honey*
*grated rind and juice of 1 orange*
*1 aubergine*
*4 tomatoes, peeled and chopped*
*115g/4oz/½ cup ready-to-eat dried apricots, halved*
*30ml/2 tbsp chopped fresh coriander*
*salt and freshly ground black pepper*

FOR THE COUSCOUS
*225g/8oz/1⅓ cups couscous*
*pinch of saffron strands, soaked in 15ml/1 tbsp boiling water (optional)*
*knob of butter*
*5ml/1 tsp orange flower water (optional)*

SERVES 4

1 Heat the oil in a large pan or flameproof casserole. Add the lamb and onion and sauté for 5 minutes until lightly browned.

2 Add the garlic, then stir in the stock, cinnamon stick, fresh ginger, honey, orange rind and juice. Bring to the boil, then lower the heat, cover the pan and simmer gently for 45 minutes.

3 Meanwhile, wipe the aubergine and cut into pieces. Place in a mixing bowl and sprinkle with 30–45ml/2–3 tbsp salt. Leave for about 30 minutes so that the bitter juices are drawn out.

4 Add the chopped tomatoes and dried apricots to the casserole. Rinse the aubergines, drain well and add to the tagine. Cover and cook for 45 minutes more, or until the lamb is tender.

5 About 20 minutes before the lamb is ready, cook the couscous, either in a separate pan or in a steamer above the stew. Start by placing the couscous in a bowl, pour over lightly salted boiling water to cover and sprinkle with the infused saffron, if using. Soak for 5 minutes. Place the butter in a saucepan, add the couscous and cook over a moderate heat for 3–5 minutes. Alternatively, place the couscous in a steamer set above the stew and steam it for 6–7 minutes. Tip the couscous into a mixing bowl and sprinkle with orange flower water, if using.

6 Stir the fresh coriander into the tagine just before serving with the couscous.

# CHICKEN WITH PRESERVED LEMON AND OLIVES

his is one of the most famous Moroccan dishes. You must use preserved lemon as fresh lemon doesn't have the mellow flavour required.

### INGREDIENTS
*30ml/2 tbsp olive oil*
*1 Spanish onion, chopped*
*3 garlic cloves*
*1cm/½in fresh root ginger, grated, or*
*2.5ml/½ tsp ground ginger*
*2.5–5ml/½–1 tsp ground cinnamon*
*pinch of saffron*
*4 chicken quarters, preferably breasts,*
*halved if liked*
*750ml/1¼ pints/3 cups chicken stock*
*30ml/2 tbsp chopped fresh coriander*
*30ml/2 tbsp chopped fresh parsley*
*1 preserved lemon, rinsed*
*115g/4oz/⅔ cup Moroccan tan olives*
*salt and freshly ground black pepper*
*lemon wedges and fresh coriander sprigs,*
*to garnish*

*SERVES 4*

1 Heat the oil in a large flameproof casserole and fry the onion for about 6–8 minutes over a moderate heat until lightly golden, stirring occasionally.

2 Crush the garlic and blend with the ginger, cinnamon, saffron and a little salt and pepper. Stir into the pan and fry for 1 minute. Add the chicken and fry for about 2–3 minutes until lightly browned.

3 Add the stock, coriander and parsley, bring to the boil, cover and simmer for 45 minutes until the chicken is tender.

4 Discard the flesh of the preserved lemon and cut the peel into small pieces. Stir into the pan with the olives and simmer for 15 minutes until the chicken is very tender. Transfer the chicken to a plate and keep warm. Bring the sauce to the boil and cook for 3–4 minutes until reduced and thick.

5 Pour the sauce over the chicken and serve with lemon wedges and coriander.

### PRESERVED LEMONS
Quarter 5 lemons lengthways, to within 1cm/½in of the bottom. Weigh out 65g/2½oz salt. Sprinkle the lemon flesh with some of the salt and reshape. Place 30ml/2 tbsp of the salt in a sterilized jar and press in the lemons, sprinkling over the remaining salt. Push down so that the lemons release their juice, then pour in enough lemon juice to cover the fruit completely. Leave for 20–30 days, shaking the jar every other day.

# BEEF TAGINE WITH SWEET POTATOES

T agines, by definition, are cooked on the hob (or over coals in Morocco), but this recipe works in the oven.

### INGREDIENTS
*675–900g/1½–2lb braising or stewing beef*
*30ml/2 tbsp sunflower oil*
*good pinch of ground turmeric*
*1 large onion, chopped*
*1 red or green chilli, seeded and chopped*
*7.5ml/1½ tsp paprika*
*good pinch of cayenne pepper*
*2.5ml/½ tsp ground cumin*
*450g/1lb sweet potatoes*
*15ml/1 tbsp chopped fresh parsley, plus*
*extra to garnish*
*15ml/1 tbsp chopped fresh coriander*
*15g/½oz/1 tbsp butter*
*salt and freshly ground black pepper*

*SERVES 4*

1 Trim the meat and cut into 2cm/¾in cubes. Heat the oil and fry the meat, together with the turmeric and seasoning, over a medium heat for 3–4 minutes until evenly brown, stirring frequently. Cover the pan and cook for 15 minutes over a gentle heat, without lifting the lid. Preheat the oven to 180°C/350°F/Gas 4.

2 Add the onion, chilli, paprika, cayenne pepper and cumin to the pan with just enough water to cover the meat. Cover tightly and cook in the oven for 1–1½ hours until the meat is very tender, adding a little extra water to keep the stew fairly moist.

3 Peel the sweet potatoes and slice into a bowl of salted water, as they discolour quickly. Transfer to a pan, bring to the boil and simmer for 2–3 minutes. Drain well.

4 Stir the herbs into the meat, adding a little water if needed. Arrange the potato slices over the meat and dot with butter. Cover and cook in the oven for 10 minutes or until the potatoes feel very tender.

5 Increase the oven temperature to 200°C/400°F/Gas 6 or heat the grill. Remove the lid and cook for 5–10 minutes until the potatoes are golden. Serve garnished with freshly chopped parsley.

# SEVEN-VEGETABLE COUSCOUS

even is a magical number in Morocco and there are many recipes for this glorious celebration couscous. The vegetables here are carrots, parsnips, turnips, onions, courgettes, tomatoes and French beans. You could substitute different vegetables if you wish.

### INGREDIENTS

*30ml/2 tbsp sunflower oil or olive oil*
*450g/1lb lean lamb, cut into*
*bite-size pieces*
*2 chicken breast quarters, halved*
*2 onions, chopped*
*350g/12oz carrots, cut into chunks*
*225g/8oz parsnips, cut into chunks*
*115g/4oz turnips, cut into cubes*
*6 tomatoes, peeled and chopped*
*900ml/1½ pints/3¾ cups chicken stock*
*good pinch of ground ginger*
*1 cinnamon stick*
*400g/14oz can chick-peas, drained*
*400g/14oz/2⅓ cups couscous*
*2 small courgettes, cut into julienne strips*
*115g/4oz French beans, trimmed and*
*halved if necessary*
*50g/2oz/⅓ cup raisins*
*a little harissa or Tabasco sauce*
*salt and freshly ground black pepper*

*SERVES 6*

1 Heat half the oil in a large saucepan or flameproof casserole and fry the lamb pieces, in batches if necessary, until evenly browned, stirring frequently. Transfer the lamb to a plate with a slotted spoon. Add the chicken pieces and cook until they are evenly browned. Transfer to the plate with the lamb.

2 Heat the remaining oil and add the chopped onions. Fry over a gentle heat for 2–3 minutes, stirring occasionally, then add the chopped carrots, parsnips and turnips. Stir well, cover with a lid and "sweat" over a gentle heat for 5–6 minutes, stirring once or twice.

3 Add the tomatoes, lamb, chicken and stock. Season to taste with salt and black pepper and add the ground ginger and the cinnamon stick. Bring to the boil and simmer gently for 35–45 minutes until the meat is nearly tender.

4 Skin the chick-peas by placing them in a bowl of cold water and rubbing them between your fingers. The skins will rise to the surface. Discard the skins and drain. Prepare the couscous according to the instructions on the packet.

5 Add the chick-peas, courgettes, beans and raisins to the meat mixture, stir and continue cooking for 10–15 minutes until the vegetables and meat are tender. Pile the couscous on to a large serving platter, making a slight well in the centre.

6 Transfer the chicken to a plate and remove the skin and bone, if you wish. Spoon 3–4 large spoonfuls of stock from the stew into a separate saucepan. Stir the chicken back into the stew, add harissa or Tabasco sauce to the separate stock and heat both gently. Spoon the stew over the couscous. Serve the harissa sauce in a separate bowl.

# TROUT WITH FILO PASTRY AND ALMOND CRUST

rapped in filo pastry and filled with an almond stuffing, trout is transformed into a special dish that makes a filling main course for any party meal.

### INGREDIENTS
*4 trout, about 175g/6oz each, gutted*
*75g/3oz/6 tbsp butter*
*1 small onion, finely chopped*
*30ml/2 tbsp chopped fresh parsley*
*finely grated rind of 1 lemon*
*115g/4oz/1 cup ground almonds*
*12 sheets of filo pastry*
*salt and freshly ground black pepper*
*lemon slices and fresh parsley sprigs,*
*to garnish*

### SERVES 4

1 Preheat the oven to 200°C/400°F/Gas 6. Season the trout well.

2 Melt 25g/1oz/2 tbsp of the butter in a large, heavy-based saucepan and cook the onion until soft but not coloured.

3 Add the parsley, lemon rind and 75g/3oz/¾ cup of the ground almonds. Stuff each fish with the mixture.

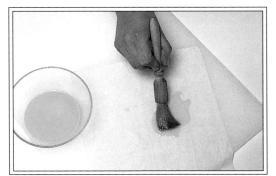

4 Melt the remaining butter. Cut the filo pastry into strips and brush each one with the butter.

5 Wrap the strips around each fish to enclose it completely. Place them on a baking sheet.

6 Sprinkle the remaining ground almonds evenly over the top of the pastry and bake the fish in the preheated oven for about 20–25 minutes until the pastry strips turn golden brown. Serve the trout garnished with slices of lemon and some fresh sprigs of parsley.

# FISH CUTLETS

delicious summer dish, perfect when served with a simple salad or warm Moroccan bread.

### INGREDIENTS
*4 white fish cutlets, about 150g/5oz each*
*about 150ml/¼ pint/⅔ cup fish stock,*
*for poaching*
*1 bay leaf*
*a few black peppercorns*
*a strip of pared lemon rind*
*lemon wedges and fresh parsley sprigs,*
*to garnish*

### FOR THE TOMATO SAUCE
*400g/14oz can chopped tomatoes*
*1 garlic clove, crushed*
*15ml/1 tbsp sun-dried tomato paste*
*15ml/1 tbsp drained capers*
*12–16 stoned black olives*
*salt and freshly ground black pepper*

### SERVES 4

1 Gently heat together all the tomato sauce ingredients in a saucepan with 15ml/1 tbsp water.

2 Place the fish in a frying pan and add the fish stock, bay leaf, peppercorns and lemon rind.

3 Cover and simmer the fish and other ingredients for 10 minutes, or until the fish flakes easily.

4 Using a slotted spoon, transfer the fish to a heated dish. Strain the stock into the tomato sauce and boil until it has reduced slightly in quantity.

5 Season the tomato sauce, pour it over the fish and serve immediately, garnished with lemon wedges and some fresh sprigs of parsley.

# SEA BREAM WITH ARTICHOKES AND COURGETTES

he distinctive charmoula marinade gives this baked fish dish a truly irresistible flavour.

### INGREDIENTS
*1–2 whole sea bream or sea bass, about*
*1.5kg/3–3½lb, cleaned and scaled, with*
*the head and tail left on*
*2 onions*
*2–3 courgettes*
*4 tomatoes*
*45ml/3 tbsp olive oil*
*5ml/1 tsp fresh thyme*
*400g/14oz can artichoke hearts*
*lemon wedges and finely pared rind,*
*salt*
*black olives and fresh coriander leaves,*
*to garnish*

### FOR THE CHARMOULA
*1 onion, chopped*
*2 garlic cloves, halved*
*½ bunch fresh parsley*
*3–4 fresh coriander sprigs*
*pinch of paprika*
*45ml/3 tbsp olive oil*
*30ml/2 tbsp white wine vinegar*
*15ml/1 tbsp lemon juice*
*salt and freshly ground black pepper*

*SERVES 4*

1 To make the charmoula, place all the ingredients in a food processor or blender with 45ml/3 tbsp water and process until the onion is finely chopped and the ingredients are all well combined. Alternatively, chop the onion, garlic and herbs finely and blend with the other ingredients and the water.

2 Make three or four slashes on both sides of the fish. Place in a bowl and spread with the charmoula, pressing it into both sides of the fish. Set aside for 2–3 hours, turning the fish occasionally.

3 Slice the onions. Top and tail the courgettes and cut into julienne strips. Peel the tomatoes, discard the seeds and chop roughly.

4 Preheat the oven to 220°C/425°F/Gas 7. Place the sliced onions, courgettes and tomatoes in the bottom of a shallow ovenproof dish. Sprinkle them well with olive oil, salt and fresh thyme and roast in the oven for 15–20 minutes, until the vegetables are softened and slightly charred, stirring occasionally.

5 Reduce the oven temperature to 180°C/350°F/Gas 4. Add the artichoke hearts to the dish and place the fish, together with the charmoula marinade, on top of the roasted vegetables. Pour over 150ml/¼ pint/⅔ cup water and cover the dish with foil.

6 Bake for 30–35 minutes or until the fish is tender. (It will depend on whether you are cooking 1 large or 2 smaller fish.) For the last 5 minutes of cooking, remove the foil to allow the skin to brown lightly. Alternatively, place the fish under a hot grill and grill for 2–3 minutes.

7 Arrange the cooked fish on a large warmed serving platter and spoon the roasted vegetables around the sides. Garnish the fish with lemon wedges and finely pared strips of lemon rind, black olives and fresh coriander leaves before serving.

# RED MULLET WITH CUMIN

colourful combination of tomatoes, parsley and red mullet, quick to prepare and simple to cook under a grill or on the barbecue.

### INGREDIENTS
*8–12 red mullet, depending on size of fish, cleaned, scaled and with heads removed if liked*
*fresh parsley and finely pared strips of lemon rind, to garnish*

### FOR THE CHARMOULA
*10ml/2 tsp ground cumin*
*5ml/1 tsp paprika*
*60ml/4 tbsp lemon juice*
*45ml/3 tbsp olive oil*
*30ml/2 tbsp chopped fresh parsley*
*salt and freshly ground black pepper*

### FOR THE FRESH TOMATO SAUCE
*5 large tomatoes*
*2 garlic cloves, chopped*
*60ml/4 tbsp chopped fresh parsley and coriander*
*30ml/2 tbsp olive oil*
*30ml/2 tbsp lemon juice*

*SERVES 4*

1 Make 2–3 slashes along the sides of the fish and place in a dish. Blend together the charmoula ingredients and rub into the fish on both sides. Set aside for 2 hours.

2 To make the fresh tomato sauce, peel the tomatoes and cut into small pieces, discarding the core and seeds. Place in a mixing bowl and stir in the remaining ingredients. Set aside in the fridge or a cool place until needed.

3 Heat the grill or prepare the barbecue. Grill or barbecue the fish for 5–6 minutes on each side, until the flesh is tender. Garnish with fresh parsley and lemon rind and serve immediately with the chilled fresh tomato sauce.

# FISH BROCHETTES

These white fish skewers make good summer barbecue food and the charmoula marinade evokes the tastes and smells of a Moroccan evening.

INGREDIENTS
*450g/1lb white fish fillets, such as cod,*
*haddock, monkfish or sea bass*
*olive oil, for brushing*
*chopped fresh parsley, to garnish*
*lime wedges, to serve*

FOR THE CHARMOULA
*½ onion, grated or very finely chopped*
*2 garlic cloves, crushed*
*30ml/2 tbsp chopped fresh coriander*
*15ml/1 tbsp chopped fresh parsley*
*5ml/1 tsp ground cumin*
*10ml/2 tsp paprika*
*good pinch of ground ginger*
*25ml/1½ tbsp white wine vinegar*
*30ml/2 tbsp lime juice*
*salt and pinch of cayenne pepper*

SERVES 4

1 To make the charmoula marinade, blend together all the ingredients in a bowl and season to taste with salt and a pinch of cayenne pepper.

2 Cut the fish into 1cm/½in cubes, discarding any skin and bones. Place in a shallow dish and add the charmoula, stirring to ensure all the fish is coated thoroughly. Cover with clear film and set aside for about 2 hours.

3 Prepare the barbecue or preheat the grill. Thread the fish on to twelve small or eight large wooden or metal kebab skewers. Brush with a little olive oil.

4 Cook the kebabs for 7–10 minutes until the fish is cooked through, turning and brushing with more olive oil occasionally. Garnish the kebabs with chopped fresh parsley and serve along with some wedges of lime.

# MONKFISH WITH PEPPERED CITRUS MARINADE

onkfish is a firm, meaty fish that keeps its shape well. Serve this dish with a crisp green salad.

INGREDIENTS

*2 monkfish tails, about 350g/12oz each*
*1 lime*
*1 lemon*
*2 oranges*
*handful of fresh thyme sprigs*
*30ml/2 tbsp olive oil*
*15ml/1 tbsp mixed peppercorns,*
*roughly crushed*
*salt and freshly ground black pepper*

SERVES 4

1 Remove any skin from the monkfish tails. Cut carefully down one side of the backbone, sliding a sharp knife between the bone and flesh, to remove the fillet on one side. You can ask your fishmonger to do this for you.

2 Turn the fish over and repeat on the other side, to remove the second fillet. Repeat on the second tail. Lay the four fillets out flat.

3 Using a sharp knife, cut two slices each from the lime, lemon and orange and arrange them over two of the fish fillets. Add a few sprigs of fresh thyme and sprinkle with salt and pepper. Finely grate the rind from the remaining fruit and sprinkle it over the fish.

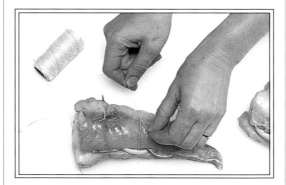

4 Lay the other two fish fillets on top and tie them firmly at intervals, with fine cotton string, to hold them in shape. Place in a wide dish.

5 Squeeze the juice from the citrus fruits and mix with the oil and more salt and pepper. Spoon over the fish. Cover and leave to marinate for 1 hour, turning occasionally and spooning the marinade over it.

6 Drain the monkfish, reserving the marinade, and sprinkle with the crushed peppercorns. Cook under a medium-hot grill for 20–25 minutes, basting with the marinade and turning occasionally, until evenly cooked.

# SPICED ROAST POUSSIN

A very tasty spiced yogurt and rice stuffing is what gives the poussin its subtle flavour here.

### INGREDIENTS
*75g/3oz/1 cup cooked long grain rice*
*1 small onion, chopped finely*
*finely grated rind and juice of 1 lemon*
*30ml/2 tbsp chopped fresh mint*
*45ml/3 tbsp chopped ready-to-eat dried apricots*
*30ml/2 tbsp natural yogurt*
*10ml/2 tsp ground turmeric*
*10ml/2 tsp ground cumin*
*2 poussin, each 450g/1lb*
*salt and freshly ground black pepper*
*lemon slices and mint sprigs, to garnish*

### SERVES 4

1 Preheat the oven to 200°C/400°F/Gas 6. Mix together the rice, onion, lemon rind, mint and apricots. Stir in half each of the lemon juice, yogurt, turmeric and cumin, and salt and pepper to taste.

2 Stuff the poussin with the rice mixture at the neck end only. Any spare stuffing can be served separately. Place the poussin on a rack in a roasting tin.

3 Mix together the remaining lemon juice, yogurt, turmeric and cumin, then brush this over the poussin. Cover loosely with foil and cook in the oven for 30 minutes.

4 Remove the foil and roast for a further 15 minutes, or until golden brown and the juices run clear when pierced.

5 Cut the poussin in half with a sharp knife or poultry shears, and serve with the reserved rice. Garnish with lemon slices and fresh mint.

# PAN-FRIED CHICKEN

The essence of this dish is to cook it quickly over a fierce heat, and it therefore works best with small quantities. Served with bread, this dish also makes an excellent first course.

### INGREDIENTS
*2 skinned and boned chicken breasts*
*1 small red or green chilli, seeded and finely sliced*
*2 garlic cloves, finely sliced*
*3 spring onions, sliced*
*4–5 wafer-thin slices fresh root ginger*
*2.5ml/½ tsp ground coriander*
*2.5ml/½ tsp ground cumin*
*30ml/2 tbsp olive oil plus extra, for frying*
*25ml/1½ tbsp lemon juice*
*30ml/2 tbsp pine nuts*
*15ml/1 tbsp raisins (optional)*
*15ml/1 tbsp chopped fresh coriander*
*15ml/1 tbsp chopped fresh mint*
*salt and freshly ground black pepper*
*sprigs of fresh mint and lemon slices, to garnish*
*bread, rice or couscous, to serve*

### SERVES 2

1 Cut the chicken breasts horizontally into three or four thin slices as this will speed up the cooking time. Place in a shallow bowl.

2 Blend together the chilli, garlic, spring onions, ginger, spices, 30ml/2 tbsp olive oil, lemon juice, pine nuts and raisins, if using. Season with salt and pepper and then pour over the chicken pieces, stirring so that each piece is coated. Cover with clear film and leave in a cool place for 1–2 hours.

3 Brush a wok, balti pan or cast iron frying pan with some oil and heat. Add the chicken slices and stir-fry over a fairly high heat for 3–4 minutes until the chicken is browned on both sides.

4 Add the remaining marinade and continue to cook over a high heat for 6–8 minutes or until the chicken is cooked.

5 Reduce the heat and stir in the coriander and mint. Cook for 1 minute and serve, garnished with mint sprigs and lemon slices. Serve with bread, rice or couscous.

# LAMB WITH APRICOT STUFFING

innamon and cumin make perfect partners for apricots in the bulgur wheat stuffing that fills this easy-to-carve joint.

### INGREDIENTS

*75g/3oz/½ cup bulgur wheat*
*30ml/2 tbsp olive oil*
*1 small onion, finely chopped*
*1 garlic clove, crushed*
*5ml/1 tsp ground cinnamon*
*5ml/1 tsp ground cumin*
*175g/6oz/¾ cup ready-to-eat dried apricots, chopped*
*50g/2oz/½ cup pine nuts*
*1 boned shoulder of lamb, about 1.75kg/4–4½lb*
*250ml/8fl oz/1 cup lamb stock*
*salt and freshly ground black pepper*
*mint sprigs, to garnish*

SERVES 6–8

1 Place the bulgur wheat in a bowl and cover with warm water. Leave to soak for about 1 hour, then drain thoroughly.

2 Heat the oil in a saucepan. Add the onion and garlic and cook for 5 minutes until soft. Stir in the cinnamon, cumin, apricots and pine nuts, with salt and pepper to taste. Leave the mixture aside to cool. Preheat the oven to 180°C/350°F/Gas 4.

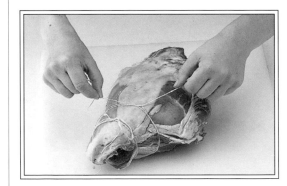

3 Open out the lamb and spread the stuffing over. Roll up firmly and tie with string.

4 Place the lamb in a roasting tin. Roast for 1 hour, then pour all of the stock into the roasting tin. Continue to roast for another 30 minutes.

5 Transfer the joint to a heated plate and cover with tented foil to allow the meat to rest. Leave aside for about 15–20 minutes before carving.

6 Meanwhile, prepare some gravy by skimming the surface fat from the stock in the roasting tin. Place the tin over a high heat and allow the gravy to bubble for a few minutes, stirring occasionally to incorporate any sediment.

7 Carve the lamb neatly, taking care that the stuffing does not crumble and fall away from the meat too much. Arrange the slices on a serving platter and pour over the gravy. Serve at once, garnished with mint.

# MOROCCAN-STYLE ROAST LAMB

L amb is by far the most favoured meat in Morocco, where whole or half lambs are still cooked over open fires. The meat is cooked in a very hot oven to start with and then finished in a cooler oven until it is so tender that it falls from the bone.

### INGREDIENTS
*1.5kg/3–3½lb leg of lamb*
*40g/1½oz/3 tbsp butter*
*2 garlic cloves, crushed*
*2.5ml/½ tsp cumin seeds*
*1.5ml/¼ tsp paprika*
*pinch of cayenne pepper*
*salt*
*fresh coriander, to garnish*
*bread or roast potatoes, to serve (optional)*

### SERVES 6

1 Trim the lamb of any excess fat and make several shallow diagonal cuts over the meat.

2 Blend together the butter, garlic, cumin, paprika, cayenne pepper and salt and spread over the surface of the lamb, pressing the mixture into the slits. Set aside for at least 2 hours or overnight.

3 Preheat the oven to 220°C/425°F/Gas 7. Place the prepared meat in a large roasting tin and cook in the centre of the oven for 15 minutes. (Be warned: the butter will burn, but the resulting flavour is delicious.) Reduce the oven temperature to 180°C/350°F/Gas 4 and continue cooking for 1½–2 hours, until the meat is well cooked and very tender, basting several times with the meat juices.

4 Place the cooked meat on a serving plate and serve immediately. In Morocco it is customary to pull the meat away from the bone using a fork, but the meat may be carved if you prefer. Garnish the lamb dish with fresh coriander and serve it Moroccan-style either with bread or with roast potatoes, if liked.

# KEBABS

This colourful Moroccan version of the famous lamb recipe can be grilled or barbecued.

### INGREDIENTS
*450g/1lb boned leg of lamb, cubed*
*1 large green pepper, seeded and cut into squares*
*1 large yellow pepper, seeded and cut into squares*
*8 baby onions, halved*
*225g/8oz button mushrooms*
*4 tomatoes, halved*
*15ml/1 tbsp melted butter*
*cooked bulgur wheat, to serve*

### FOR THE MARINADE
*45ml/3 tbsp olive oil*
*juice of 1 lemon*
*2 garlic cloves, crushed*
*1 large onion, grated*
*15ml/1 tbsp fresh oregano*
*salt and freshly ground black pepper*

### SERVES 4

1 To make the marinade, blend together the oil, lemon juice, garlic, onion, oregano and seasoning. Place the meat in a shallow dish and pour over the marinade.

2 Cover with clear film and leave to marinate overnight in the fridge.

3 Thread the cubes of lamb on to skewers, alternating with pieces of green and yellow pepper, onions and mushrooms. Thread the tomatoes on to separate skewers. Cook the kebabs and tomatoes under a hot grill for 12–15 minutes, basting with butter. Serve on a bed of bulgur wheat.

# PIGEON PIE

his recipe is based on a classic Moroccan dish called *Pastilla*, which is a filo pastry pie, filled with an unusual but delicious mixture of pigeon, eggs, spices and nuts. If pigeon is unavailable, chicken makes an equally good substitute for this pie.

INGREDIENTS

*3 pigeons*
*50g/2oz/4 tbsp butter*
*1 onion, chopped*
*1 cinnamon stick*
*2.5ml/½ tsp ground ginger*
*30ml/2 tbsp chopped fresh coriander*
*45ml/3 tbsp chopped fresh parsley*
*pinch of ground turmeric*
*15ml/1 tbsp caster sugar*
*1.5ml/¼ tsp ground cinnamon*
*115g/4oz/1 cup toasted almonds,*
*finely chopped*
*6 eggs, beaten*
*salt and freshly ground black pepper*
*cinnamon and icing sugar, for dusting*

FOR THE PASTRY
*175g/6oz/¾ cup butter, melted*
*16 sheets of filo pastry*
*1 egg yolk, for brushing*

SERVES 6

1 Wash the pigeons and place in a pan with the butter, onion, cinnamon stick, ginger, coriander, parsley and turmeric. Season with salt and pepper. Add just enough water to cover and bring to the boil. Cover and simmer gently for about 1 hour, until the pigeon flesh is very tender.

2 Strain off the pigeon stock and reserve. Skin and bone the pigeons, and shred the flesh into bite-size pieces. Preheat the oven to 180°C/350°F/Gas 4. Mix together the sugar, cinnamon and almonds in a bowl, and set aside.

3 Measure 150ml/¼ pint/⅔ cup of the reserved stock into a small saucepan. Add the beaten eggs and mix well. Stir over a low heat until the sauce turns creamy and very thick and almost set. Season with salt and pepper.

4 Brush a 30cm/12in diameter ovenproof dish with some of the melted butter and lay the first sheet of pastry in the dish. Brush this with butter and continue with five more sheets of pastry. Cover with the almond mixture, then half the egg mixture. Moisten with a little stock.

5 Layer four more sheets of filo pastry, brushing with butter as before. Lay the pigeon meat on top, then add the remaining egg mixture and more stock. Cover with all the remaining pastry, brushing each sheet with butter, and tuck in any overlap.

6 Brush the pie with egg yolk and bake in the oven for 40 minutes. Raise the oven temperature to 200°C/400°F/Gas 6, and bake for 15 minutes, until the pastry is crisp and golden. Decorate with a lattice design of cinnamon and icing sugar. Serve hot.

# SPICY BROAD BEANS

eeling the broad beans is a bit time-consuming, but well worth the effort, and this dish is so delicious that you won't want to eat broad beans any other way.

INGREDIENTS
*375g/12oz frozen broad beans*
*15g/¹⁄₂oz/1 tbsp butter*
*4–5 spring onions, sliced*
*15ml/1 tbsp chopped fresh coriander*
*5ml/1 tsp chopped fresh mint*
*2.5–5ml/¹⁄₂–1 tsp ground cumin*
*pinch of salt*
*10ml/2 tsp olive oil*

SERVES 4

1 Simmer the broad beans in water for 3–4 minutes until tender. Drain and, when cool enough to handle, peel away the outer skin, so you are left with the bright green seed.

2 Melt the butter in a small pan and gently fry the spring onions for 2–3 minutes. Add the broad beans and then stir in the coriander, mint, cumin and a pinch of salt. Stir in the olive oil and serve immediately.

# COOKED SALAD

his version of a North African favourite, *Schtada*, is served as a side dish with a main course. Make this salad the day before to improve the flavour of the vegetables.

### INGREDIENTS

*2 well-flavoured tomatoes, quartered*
*2 onions, chopped*
*½ cucumber, halved lengthways, seeded and sliced*
*1 green pepper, halved, seeded and chopped*
*30ml/2 tbsp lemon juice*
*45ml/3 tbsp olive oil*
*2 garlic cloves, crushed*
*30ml/2 tbsp chopped fresh coriander*
*salt and freshly ground black pepper*
*fresh coriander sprigs, to garnish*

*SERVES 4*

1 Put the tomatoes, onions, cucumber and green pepper into a pan, add about 60ml/4 tbsp water and simmer for a further 5 minutes. Leave aside until the vegetables have cooled.

2 Strain the vegetables and transfer to a mixing bowl. Mix the lemon juice, oil and garlic. Pour over the vegetables, season, and stir in the chopped coriander. Serve hot or chilled. Garnish with coriander sprigs.

# CHICK-PEA TAGINE

his hearty chick-pea and vegetable stew makes a filling meal. It is delicious when served with garlic-flavoured mashed potato.

### INGREDIENTS
*30ml/2 tbsp olive oil*
*1 small onion, chopped*
*225g/8oz carrots, halved and thinly sliced*
*2.5ml/½ tsp ground cumin*
*5ml/1 tsp ground coriander*
*30ml/2 tbsp plain flour*
*225g/8oz courgettes, sliced*
*200g/7oz can sweetcorn, drained*
*400g/14oz can chick-peas, drained*
*30ml/2 tbsp tomato purée*
*200ml/7fl oz/scant 1 cup hot vegetable stock*
*salt and freshly ground black pepper*
*garlic-flavoured mashed potato, to serve*

*SERVES 4*

---

### COOK'S TIP
For speedy garlic-flavoured mashed potato, simply mash potatoes with garlic butter and stir in chopped fresh parsley with a little crème fraîche.

1 Heat the oil in a frying pan. Add the onion and carrots. Toss to coat the vegetables in the oil, then cook over a moderate heat for 4 minutes.

2 Add the ground cumin, coriander and flour to the frying pan. Stir and cook for 1 minute.

3 Cut the courgette slices in half. Add to the pan with the sweetcorn, chick-peas, tomato purée and vegetable stock. Stir well. Cook for 10 minutes, stirring frequently.

4 Taste the stew and add salt and pepper. Serve at once, with garlic-flavoured mashed potato (see Cook's Tip).

# DATE, ORANGE AND CARROT SALAD

colourful and unusual salad with exotic ingredients – fresh dates and orange flower water – combined with crisp leaves, carrots, oranges and toasted almonds.

### INGREDIENTS
*1 Little Gem lettuce*
*2 carrots, finely grated*
*2 oranges*
*115g/4oz fresh dates, stoned and cut into eighths, lengthways*
*25g/1oz/¼ cup toasted whole almonds, chopped*
*30ml/2 tbsp lemon juice*
*5ml/1 tsp caster sugar*
*1.5ml/¼ tsp salt*
*15ml/1 tbsp orange flower water*

*SERVES 4*

1 Separate the lettuce leaves. Clean them thoroughly and shake dry.

2 Arrange the lettuce leaves in the bottom of a salad bowl or on individual serving plates. Place the grated carrot in a mound on top.

3 Peel and segment the orange and arrange the pieces around the carrot. Pile the dates on top, then sprinkle with the toasted almonds. Mix together the lemon juice, sugar, salt and orange flower water in a jug and sprinkle over the salad. Chill before serving.

# SPINACH WITH RAISINS AND PINE NUTS

aisins are frequently used in Moroccan recipes. Here, tossed with pine nuts, wilted spinach and croûtons, they make a delicious snack or main meal accompaniment.

INGREDIENTS
*50g/2oz/⅓ cup raisins*
*1 thick slice crusty white bread*
*45ml/3 tbsp olive oil*
*25g/1oz/⅓ cup pine nuts*
*500g/1¼lb young spinach, stalks removed*
*2 garlic cloves, crushed*
*salt and freshly ground black pepper*

SERVES 4

COOK'S TIP
Use Swiss chard or spinach beet instead of the spinach if you like, but make sure that they are cooked a little longer.

1 Put the raisins in a small mixing bowl with boiling water and leave to soak for 10 minutes. Drain.

2 For the croûtons, cut the bread into cubes and discard the crusts. Heat 30ml/2 tbsp of the oil, fry until golden and drain.

3 Heat the remaining oil in the pan. Fry the pine nuts until beginning to colour. Add the spinach and garlic and cook quickly, turning the spinach until it has just wilted.

4 Toss in the raisins and season lightly with salt and pepper. Transfer to a warmed serving dish. Scatter with the croûtons and serve hot.

# LITTLE SPICED BREADS

hese rich breads are given a distinctly Moroccan flavour by the addition of orange flower water.

### INGREDIENTS
*5ml/1 tsp sugar*
*10ml/2 tsp dried yeast*
*75g/3oz/6 tbsp butter, melted*
*15ml/1 tbsp orange flower water or*
*almond essence (optional)*
*400g/14oz/3½ cups strong white flour*
*75g/3oz/¾ cup icing sugar*
*5ml/1 tsp salt*
*30ml/2 tbsp sesame seeds*
*15ml/1 tbsp fennel seeds*
*1 egg, beaten with 15ml/1 tbsp water*

*MAKES 12*

---

#### COOK'S TIP
Once baked, these spicy breads are best served with butter and honey – choose a fragrant variety of honey.

---

1 Place 120ml/4fl oz/½ cup warm water in a jug, stir in the sugar and sprinkle the dried yeast on top. Stir and then set aside for about 10 minutes until frothy.

2 Place the melted butter together with the orange flower water or almond essence, if using, in a separate jug. Pour in about 175ml/6fl oz/¾ cup warm water and stir to mix.

3 Stir the flour, icing sugar, salt, sesame seeds and fennel seeds together in the bowl of a food processor or blender fitted with the dough blade.

4 Add the yeast and half of the butter and water mixture to the flour in the food processor or blender and process so that the ingredients slowly combine. Continue processing, adding the remaining butter and water to make a smooth and glossy dough. (You may need to add extra flour or warm water to get the right consistency.)

5 Continue processing the bread dough for about 1–2 minutes, then transfer it to a floured board or work surface and knead by hand for a few minutes until the dough is smooth and elastic.

6 Place the dough in a clean, lightly oiled bowl, cover with clear film and leave in a warm place for 1–1½ hours until doubled in size. Knead again for a few minutes and then break into twelve small balls and flatten slightly with oiled hands. Place on a greased baking tray, cover with oiled clear film and leave to rise for 1 hour.

7 Preheat the oven to 190°C/375°F/Gas 5. Brush the breads with the beaten egg and bake in the oven for 12–15 minutes or until golden brown. Serve warm or cold.

# MOROCCAN BREAD

 arm this bread in the oven and cut it into thick slices to serve with any classic Moroccan savoury dish – just the thing for mopping up a really tasty sauce.

## INGREDIENTS
*275g/10oz/2½ cups strong white flour*
*175g/6oz/1½ cups wholemeal flour*
*10ml/2 tsp salt*
*about 250ml/8fl oz/1 cup warm milk and water, mixed*
*10ml/2 tsp sesame seeds*

## FOR THE YEAST STARTER
*150ml/¼ pint/⅔ cup warm milk and water, mixed*
*5ml/1 tsp sugar*
*10ml/2 tsp dried yeast*

*MAKES 2 LOAVES*

1 To prepare the yeast, place the warm milk mixture in a jug, stir in the sugar and sprinkle with the yeast. Stir and leave in a warm place for 10 minutes until frothy.

2 In a large mixing bowl, mix together the two flours and salt. Add the yeast mixture and enough warm milk and water to make a fairly soft dough.

3 Knead the mixture into a ball and then knead on a floured work surface or board for 10–12 minutes until the dough is firm and elastic. Break into two and shape each piece into a flattened ball shape. Place them on floured baking trays.

4 Press down with your hand on each ball so that they are 13–15cm/5–6in in diameter. Cover the breads with oiled clear film or a clean, damp dish towel and set aside for 1–1½ hours in a warm place until risen. The breads are ready to bake when the dough springs back when gently pressed with a finger.

5 Preheat the oven to 200°C/400°F/Gas 6. Sprinkle the loaves with the sesame seeds and bake for 12 minutes. Reduce the oven temperature to 150°C/300°F/Gas 2 and continue baking the loaves for another 20–30 minutes until they are golden brown and sound hollow when tapped.

# SPICED HONEY NUT CAKE

**A** combination of ground pistachio nuts and breadcrumbs replaces flour in this recipe, to make a light, moist sponge cake.

### INGREDIENTS
*115g/4oz/ generous ½ cup caster sugar*
*4 eggs, separated*
*grated rind and juice of 1 lemon*
*115g/4oz/1 cup ground pistachio nuts,*
*plus extra for sprinkling*
*50g/2oz/scant 1 cup dried breadcrumbs*

### FOR THE GLAZE
*1 lemon*
*90ml/6 tbsp clear honey*
*1 cinnamon stick*

### SERVES 9

**1** Preheat the oven to 180°C/350°F/Gas 4. Grease and base-line a 20cm/8in square cake tin.

**2** Beat the sugar, egg yolks, lemon rind and juice together until pale and creamy. Fold in the pistachio nuts and breadcrumbs.

**3** Whisk the egg whites until stiff and fold into the creamed mixture. Place in the cake tin and bake for 15 minutes until risen.

**4** Cool in the cake tin for 10 minutes, then transfer to a wire rack. For the glaze, peel the lemon and cut the rind into thin strips. Squeeze the juice into a saucepan and add the honey and cinnamon stick. Bring to the boil, add the shredded rind, and simmer fast for 1 minute. Allow to cool.

**5** Place the cake on a serving plate, prick all over with a skewer, and pour over the cooled mixture. Sprinkle over the pistachios.

# SERPENT CAKE

his is perhaps the most famous of all Moroccan pastries, filled with a lightly fragrant almond paste.

INGREDIENTS
*8 sheets of filo pastry*
*50g/2oz/4 tbsp butter, melted*
*1 egg, beaten*
*5ml/1 tsp ground cinnamon*
*icing sugar, for dusting*

FOR THE ALMOND PASTE
*about 50g/2oz/4 tbsp butter, melted*
*225g/8oz/2 cups ground almonds*
*2.5ml/½ tsp almond essence*
*1 egg yolk, beaten*
*50g/2oz/½ cup icing sugar*
*15ml/1 tbsp rose water or orange flower water (optional)*

SERVES 8

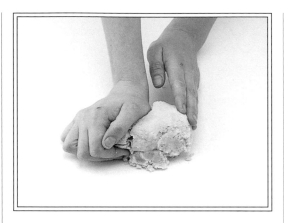

1 To make the almond paste, blend the melted butter with the ground almonds and almond essence. Add the egg yolk, icing sugar and rose or orange flower water, if using. Mix well and knead until soft and pliable. Leave in a cool place to chill for about 10 minutes.

2 Break the almond paste into ten even-size balls and then roll them into 10cm/4in "sausages". Chill once more.

3 Preheat the oven to 180°C/350°F/Gas 4. Place two sheets of filo pastry on the work surface or a board so that they overlap to form a 18 x 56cm/7 x 22in rectangle. Brush the overlapping pastry to secure and then brush all over with butter. Cover with another two sheets of filo and brush again with butter.

4 Place five "sausages" of almond paste along the lower edge of the filo sheet and roll up the pastry tightly, tucking in the ends. Shape the roll into a loose coil. Repeat with the remaining filo and almond paste, so that you have two coils.

5 Brush a baking sheet with butter. Place the coils together to make a "snake".

6 Beat together the egg and half of the cinnamon. Brush over the "snake" and then bake in the oven for 20–25 minutes until golden brown. Carefully invert the "snake" on to a baking sheet and return to the oven for 5–10 minutes until golden.

7 Place on a serving plate. Dust with icing sugar and then sprinkle with the remaining cinnamon. Serve warm.

# BRIOUATES WITH ALMONDS AND DATES

It is worth investing in a good-quality honey to dip these delicious pastries into – it makes all the difference to the final result.

### INGREDIENTS
*15ml/1 tbsp sunflower oil*
*225g/8oz/1⅓ cups blanched almonds*
*115g/4oz/⅔ cup stoned dates*
*25g/1oz/2 tbsp butter, softened*
*5ml/1 tsp ground cinnamon*
*1.5ml/¼ tsp almond essence*
*40g/1½oz/⅓ cup icing sugar*
*30ml/2 tbsp orange flower water or
rose water*
*10 sheets of filo pastry*
*50g/2oz/4 tbsp melted butter*
*120ml/4fl oz/½ cup fragrant honey
dates, to serve*

*MAKES ABOUT 30*

1 Heat the oil in a small pan and fry the almonds for a few minutes until golden, stirring all the time. Drain on kitchen paper to cool, then grind in a coffee or spice mill. Pound the dates by hand or process in a blender or food processor. Preheat the oven to 180°C/350°F/Gas 4.

2 Put the ground almonds into a bowl or into the blender or food processor with the dates and process with the butter, cinnamon, almond essence, icing sugar and some orange flower or rose water to taste. If the mixture is stiff, add more flower water.

3 Brush a sheet of filo pastry with melted butter and cut into three equal strips, keeping the remaining sheets covered with clear film to prevent them drying out.

4 Place a walnut-size piece of paste at the bottom of each strip. Fold a corner over the filling to make a triangle and then fold up, in triangles, to make a neat package.

5 Brush the package with a little butter, then repeat steps 3 and 4 to make about 30 pastries. Place the pastries on a buttered baking sheet and bake for 30 minutes until golden. If possible, cook in batches, as once cooked they are immediately immersed in the honey.

6 While the Briouates are cooking, pour the honey and a little more of the orange flower or rose water into a pan and heat gently. When the pastries are cooked, lower them one by one into the pan and turn them in the honey mixture so that they are thoroughly coated. Transfer to a plate and cool a little before serving with dates.

# ALMOND CAKE

**T**his is a truly delicious cake that makes excellent use of one of Morocco's most popular ingredients, almonds. It can be served for breakfast with a refreshing cup of mint tea, or as a nice snack in the afternoon.

### INGREDIENTS
250g/9oz/1½ cups blanched almonds
25g/1oz/2 tbsp butter
75g/3oz/¾ icing sugar
3 eggs
2.5ml/½ tsp almond extract
25g/1oz/¼ cup flour
3 egg whites
15ml/1 tbsp granulated sugar
toasted almonds, to decorate

### SERVES 4–6

1 Preheat the oven to 160°C/325°F/Gas 3. Line a 23cm/9in round cake tin with greaseproof paper and grease.

2 Spread the almonds on a baking tray and bake in the oven for 10 minutes, until golden. Cool, then roughly chop them.

3 Melt the butter and set aside. Raise the oven temperature to 200°C/400°F/Gas 6.

4 Grind the toasted chopped almonds with half the icing sugar in a food processor, blender or a nut grinder.

5 Transfer the ground nuts and icing sugar to a mixing bowl. Add the whole eggs and remaining icing sugar. With an electric mixer, beat until the mixture forms a ribbon when the beaters are lifted. Mix in the butter and almond extract. Sift over the flour and fold in gently.

6 With an electric mixer, beat the egg whites until they hold soft peaks. Add the sugar and beat until stiff and glossy.

7 Fold the whites into the almond mixture in four batches.

8 Spoon the batter into the tin and bake in the centre of the oven until golden brown, about 15–20 minutes. Decorate with toasted almonds and serve warm.

# RICE PUDDING

simple and delicious alternative to a traditional rice pudding. The rice is cooked in almond-flavoured milk and delicately flavoured with cinnamon and orange flower water.

### INGREDIENTS
*25g/1oz/¼ cup blanched*
*almonds, chopped*
*450g/1lb/2¼ cups pudding rice*
*25g/1oz/¼ cup icing sugar*
*7.5cm/3in cinnamon stick*
*50g/2oz/¼ cup butter*
*pinch of salt*
*1.5ml/¼ tsp almond essence*
*175ml/6fl oz/¾ cup condensed milk*
*175ml/6fl oz/¾ cup milk*
*30ml/2 tbsp orange flower water*
*toasted flaked almonds and ground*
*cinnamon, to decorate*

### SERVES 6

1 Put the chopped almonds in a food processor or blender along with 60ml/4 tbsp very hot water. Process, then push through a sieve into a mixing bowl.

2 Return the almond mixture to the food processor or blender, add a further 60ml/4 tbsp very hot water, and repeat.

3 Add 300ml/½ pint/1¼ cups water to the almond "milk" in the saucepan and bring to the boil. Add the pudding rice, icing sugar, cinnamon stick and half the butter, the salt, the almond essence, the condensed milk and half the milk.

4 Bring the mixture to the boil, then simmer, covered, for about 30 minutes, adding more milk if necessary. Continue to cook the rice, stirring and adding the remaining milk, until it is thick and creamy. Stir in the flower water, then taste for sweetness, adding extra sugar, if necessary.

5 Pour the rice pudding into a serving bowl, and sprinkle with the flaked almonds. Dot with the remaining butter and dust with ground cinnamon. Serve hot.

# YOGURT WITH APRICOTS AND PISTACHIOS

f you allow a thick yogurt to drain overnight, it becomes even thicker and more luscious. Add honeyed apricots and nuts and you have an exotic yet simple dessert.

### INGREDIENTS
*450g/1lb natural yogurt*
*175g/6oz/²⁄₃ cup ready-to-eat dried apricots, snipped*
*15ml/1 tbsp honey*
*grated rind of 1 orange*
*30ml/2 tbsp unsalted pistachio nuts, roughly chopped*
*ground cinnamon, to decorate*

SERVES 4

---

COOK'S TIP
For a simple dessert, strain the fruit, then cover with yogurt and sprinkle with brown sugar and a little allspice or cinnamon.

---

1 Place the natural yogurt in a fine sieve and allow it to drain overnight in the fridge over a bowl.

2 Discard the whey from the yogurt. Place the apricots in a saucepan, barely cover with water and simmer for just 3 minutes, to soften. Drain and transfer to a bowl, then mix with the honey.

3 Mix the strained yogurt with the softened apricots, orange rind and pistachio nuts. Spoon the mixture evenly into four sundae dishes, sprinkle over a little cinnamon and chill before serving.

# FILO SCRUNCHIES

**Q**uick and easy to make, these pastries are ideal to serve at tea time. Eat them warm or they will lose their crispness.

### INGREDIENTS
*5 apricots*
*4 sheets of filo pastry*
*20ml/4 tsp soft margarine, melted*
*50g/2oz/¼ cup demerara sugar*
*30ml/2 tbsp flaked almonds*
*icing sugar, to decorate*

*MAKES 6*

---

### COOK'S TIP
Filo pastry dries out very quickly once opened. Keep it covered as you work, either with a dry dish towel or some clear film to limit exposure to the air. Otherwise the pastry will become too brittle to work with.

1 Preheat the oven to 190°C/375°F/Gas 5. Halve the apricots, remove the stones and slice the fruit. Cut the sheets of filo pastry into twelve 18cm/7in squares.

2 Pile the filo squares on top of each other and cover with a clean dish towel to prevent the pastry from drying out. Remove one square of filo and brush it with melted margarine. Lay a second square on top and, using your fingers, mould the pastry into folds. Make five more scrunchies, working quickly so that the pastry does not dry out.

3 Arrange a few slices of fruit in the folds of each scrunchie, then sprinkle generously with the demerara sugar and flaked almonds.

4 Place the scrunchies on a baking sheet and bake for 8–10 minutes until golden. Transfer the scrunchies to a wire rack. Dust with icing sugar and serve warm.

# GAZELLES' HORNS

**K**aab el Ghzal is one of Morocco's favourite and best known pastries – so popular that the French have honoured it with its own name, *Cornes de Gazelles*. The horn-shaped pastries are commonly served at wedding ceremonies.

### INGREDIENTS
*200g/7oz/1¾ cups plain flour*
*pinch of salt*
*25g/1oz/2 tbsp melted butter*
*about 30ml/2 tbsp orange flower water or water*
*1 large egg yolk, beaten*
*icing sugar, to decorate*

### FOR THE ALMOND PASTE
*200g/7oz/scant 2 cups ground almonds*
*115g/4oz/1 cup icing sugar or caster sugar*
*30ml/2 tbsp orange flower water*
*25g/1oz/2 tbsp melted butter*
*2 egg yolks, beaten*
*2.5ml/½ tsp ground cinnamon*

*MAKES ABOUT 16*

1 To make the almond paste, mix together all the ingredients in a bowl to make a smooth paste.

2 To make the pastry, mix the flour and a little salt and then stir in the melted butter, orange flower water or water, and about three-quarters of the egg yolk. Stir in cold water, little by little, to make a fairly soft dough.

3 Knead the dough for about 10 minutes until smooth and elastic, then place on a floured surface and roll out as thinly as possible. Cut the dough into long strips about 7.5cm/3in wide.

4 Preheat the oven to 180°C/350°F/Gas 4. Take small pieces of the almond paste and roll them between your hands into thin "sausages" about 7.5cm/3in long with tapering ends.

5 Place these "sausages" in a line along one side of the strips of pastry, about 3cm/1¼ in apart. Dampen the pastry edges with water and then fold the other half of the strip over the filling and press the edges together firmly.

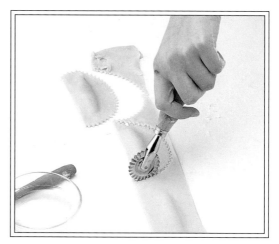

6 Using a pastry wheel, cut around each "sausage" (as you would with ravioli) to make a crescent shape. Make sure that all the edges are firmly pinched together.

7 Prick the crescents with a fork or a needle and place them on a buttered baking tray. Brush the crescents with the remaining beaten egg yolk and bake for about 12–16 minutes in the oven until lightly coloured. Cool and then dust with icing sugar.

# Index